I WANT TO DO MAGIC
Science Magic

Peter Eldin

Franklin Watts
London • Sydney

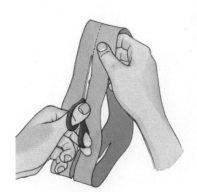

© Aladdin Books Ltd 2002
Produced by
Aladdin Books Ltd
28 Percy Street
London W1T 2BZ

ISBN 0-7496-4492–3

First published in Great Britain in 2002 by
Franklin Watts
96 Leonard Street
London EC2A 4XD

Designers:
Flick, Book Design & Graphics
Pete Bennett

Editor:
Leen De Ridder

Illustrator:
Catherine Ward – SGA

Picture Researcher:
Brian Hunter Smart

Printed in U.A.E.

A CIP catalogue record for this book is available
from the British Library.

Photo Credits:
Abbreviations: b-bottom, t-top, l-left, r-right, c-centre, m-middle.
All photos by Select Pictures,
except 26bm – Digital Stock,
31br – The Edwin A. Dawes Collection.

Contents

Introduction

Magic, the art of doing things that defy the laws of nature, appeals to people all over the world. Magic is a great hobby! Magicians through the ages have used used their knowledge of scientific principles to achieve some of their feats of mystery and to convince people that they had magical powers.

How to learn tricks

1. Read through the whole trick twice. Don't worry if you do not understand everything at this stage.

2. Gather all the things you need.

3. Go through the trick again, doing the actions step by step.

4. If you are not comfortable with a particular action, see if you can adapt it to suit you better.

5. Now practise the various movements, making sure that your hands are in the right place and that you can move smoothly from one step to another.

6. Once you have practised the moves, you can start rehearsing the trick (performing it as if for a real audience).

7. When you are happy that you can perform the trick perfectly, try it out on your friends.

DID YOU KNOW...

... that you can find lots of interesting facts about the props you use in these circles ?

Top Tip

Watch out for this symbol to read some top tips! They will help you make more of a trick or give you useful extra information.

Magicians and their magic
In boxes like this one, you will find information about famous magicians and their tricks.

IT'S **MAGIC**

SCIENCE

Are you wondering what it is that makes the tricks you do work? Then look out for this symbol! Discover the scientific principles that make the trick possible.

HINTS

• Never repeat a trick in the same company. The first showing of a trick amazes the audience. Do it again and they will know what is coming. The element of surprise will have gone and the trick will not go down so well. Because they know what is coming the second time round, it is also easier for the audience to work out how the trick is done.

• Your success as a magician will depend a lot on the way you present a trick. Even the simplest trick can look fantastic if you perform it confidently and without hesitating. This may sound like a strange piece of advice, but your performance of magic will improve if you believe that what you are doing really is magic. Believe you are doing real magic and you will be!

• When people ask how your tricks are done, do not tell them. Although many people may ask, they will be disappointed when you let them know how simple some tricks really are. Keep the secrets secret!

These exclamation marks tell you what to watch out for in certain tricks or in the preparation for them. They may look like unimportant details when you first read them, but you may give away the trick if you ignore them.

Floating metal

THE TRICK

Baffle your audience by making an everyday needle float on the surface of some water.

Preparation

You will need:
- a needle
- a glass tumbler of water
- a small piece of toilet tissue

Before you perform this trick, put the toilet tissue in your pocket. Or you may leave some tissue on the table you are using so that it will seem that a spectator trying the trick might have used some to make the trick work.

1 Show the needle and challenge a spectator to float it on the surface of the water. No matter how carefully the spectator does this, the needle will always sink to the bottom of the tumbler.

2 Now show how to do the impossible. Rest the needle on the tissue and place them on the water. Wave a magic wand or utter some magic words to enchant the needle.

IT'S MAGIc

Jailed for sorcery
Magicians through the ages have used scientific principles to achieve some of their feats of mystery. Many early scientists used their knowledge to convince people that they had magical powers, and many early magicians found that scientific discoveries could be used to make their performances even more wonderful. Sometimes, however, they scared people. Magician Andrew Oehler was jailed for sorcery in 1806 for producing ghosts at a show in Mexico.

3

When the tissue becomes soaked it will sink to the bottom of the tumbler, leaving the needle floating on the surface!

Top Tip

• *The needle must be dry for this trick to work, so when you take it from your spectator, make sure you wipe off the water.*

• *You will find that most toilet tissue has several layers, which will sink to the bottom of the glass one by one. If you think this takes too long, you can peel off one or two layers before placing the tissue on the water surface.*

SCIENCE

The needle floats because there is an invisible 'skin' on the surface of water. Water molecules are attracted to each other, and on the surface this attraction pulls the molecules close together, producing a force called surface tension. This force is strong enough to support light objects, such as a needle. The needle alone will go right through the skin, because the water molecules have no time to re-form when it pierces the surface. The water soaks through the tissue slowly, giving the water molecules time to re-form the skin.

A dicey stunt

THE TRICK

Let someone try and catch two dice in a plastic beaker. It sounds simple, but it isn't! Only you will be able to do it...

Challenge a spectator to catch two dice in a beaker. First she is to hold one die against the side of the beaker in one hand, then throw it up and catch it in the beaker. That is the easy part.

Preparation

You will need:
- 2 dice
- a plastic beaker

Then she has to put the second die on her finger just like the first one, and catch it in the beaker.

DID YOU KNOW...

... that dice are more than 2,000 years old? The ancient Greeks used dice to play games too. Of course they weren't made of plastic like today – that hadn't been invented yet. Instead, the Greeks made dice out of anklebones or shoulder blades of... sheep!

When the second die is thrown, the first one bounces out of the beaker!

4

This is how you do it. Hold one die against the side and jerk the beaker upwards. The die goes up into the air and you catch it in the beaker.

Gravity is a force that pulls everything downwards towards the Earth, including the dice in this trick.

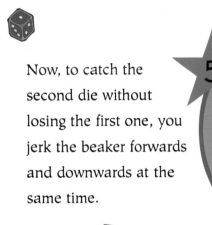

Now, to catch the second die without losing the first one, you jerk the beaker forwards and downwards at the same time.

5

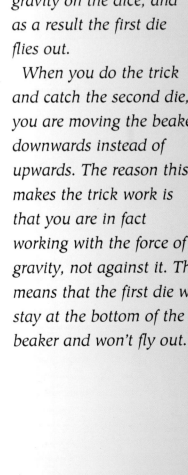

When the spectator tries to catch the second die, she is working against gravity by jerking the beaker upwards. The force of her jerking the beaker is bigger than the pull of gravity on the dice, and as a result the first die flies out.

When you do the trick and catch the second die, you are moving the beaker downwards instead of upwards. The reason this makes the trick work is that you are in fact working with the force of gravity, not against it. This means that the first die will stay at the bottom of the beaker and won't fly out.

Roses are red...

THE TRICK

In this brilliant trick, a white paper rose will slowly change colour and turn red!

Preparation

You will need:
- tissue paper
- a plastic tube
- red food colouring
- cotton wool
- thin card
- sticky tape
- green paint
- a glass or vase
- a jug of water

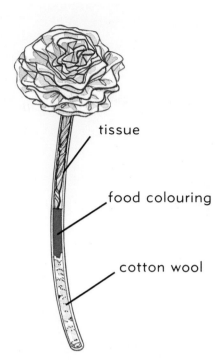

tissue

food colouring

cotton wool

1 Scrunch up the tissue paper into a rose shape and twist the corners together. Push the twist into one end of the tube.

2 Put two drops of the food colouring into the other end of the tube, then fill the rest of the tube with cotton wool.

3 Make leaves from the thin card and tape them to the tube. Paint the tube and leaves green.

4 Put the prepared flower in the vase or glass and put it on your table.

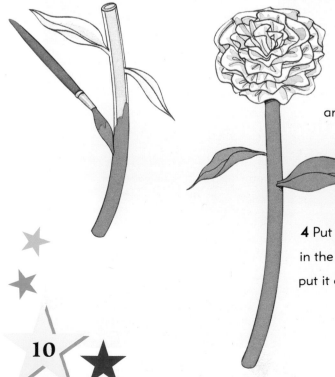

1

Show the audience the white rose and ask them what colour they think a rose should be. Someone is bound to say red.

2

Say you can make the rose change colour, but that it is quite difficult and that it will take some time. Concentrate hard, cast a spell over the rose and pour water from the jug into the vase or glass.

Top Tip

Because this trick takes a while to work, it is best to do it at the start of a show. That way you can entertain the audience with other tricks while the rose gradually changes colour. By the end of the show, your white paper rose will have turned red.

After a while the rose will have turned red, right before the audience's eyes!

SCIENCE

Plants get water from their roots to their leaves through very fine tubes in the roots, stems and branches. This absorption of water is known as capillary action. In the case of your paper rose, something similar happens. There are thousands of tiny spaces between the fibres of the cotton wool and tissue paper – this is where the water is drawn up. The water is gradually absorbed into the cotton wool and then up into the tissue paper. The food colouring mixes with the water and is carried into the flower. You can find another trick based on capillary action on page 15.

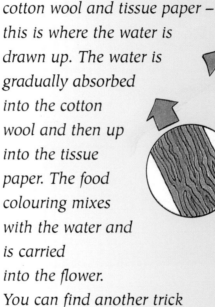

3

Long and short

THE TRICK

Your audience will rub their eyes in disbelief at this trick! You show them some strips of paper, and although they would swear they know which one is longest, you will prove them wrong!

Preparation

You will need:
- white paper
- black paper
- scissors

From the sheet of white paper cut three strips of equal length. One strip should be about half the width of the other two.

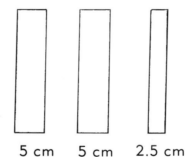

5 cm   5 cm   2.5 cm

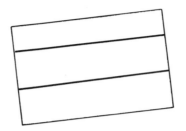

Place the three strips of paper on the black paper in the arrangement shown in step 1. Ask a spectator to choose which strip of paper is longest but to keep the answer secret.

Now ask him to look away for a moment while you rearrange the strips as in step 2. Ask him again to decide which strip he thinks is the longest, the thin one or one of the thick ones.

DID YOU KNOW...

... that your eyes can trick you and put this boy back together? Look at the space between the boy's top and bottom half. Move the page closer to your eyes, and the boy will be joined back together!

3

Now rearrange the strips one last time while the spectator is not looking, and ask the same question. This time he can say his answer out loud.

To the spectator the thinnest strip appears to be the longest. Take the three strips off the black paper and hold them together. Your spectator will be amazed to see that they are all of the same length.

4

SCIENCE

As you look down a long, straight road, you see that it seems to grow narrower in the distance (see below). Trees and telephone poles along the road appear to grow smaller as they stretch away towards the horizon. A person wearing a suit with up-and-down stripes looks thinner than he would if the stripes went crosswise. We call these kinds of appearances optical illusions.

In the trick, something similar happens: our eyes deceive us, because it seems as if the thinner strip of paper is longer than the other two. When you hold them next to each other, it becomes clear that in fact they are all the same length.

The trick on page 14 is also an optical illusion.

13

Changing colours

The Trick

Black and white card circles rest on squares of the opposite colour. It appears that the white circle is the larger of the two, but when you hold the circles together, spectators will be amazed to see that they are exactly the same size.

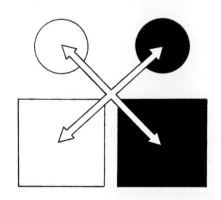

Preparation

You will need:
• black and white card squares, each 30 cm on a side.
• black and white card circles, each 15 cm across.

1 Put the white circle on the black square.
2 Put the black circle on the white square.

Show the audience the two circles resting on squares of the opposite colour and ask which of the circles is larger. The spectators will agree that the white circle is larger than the black circle.

Pick up the two circles and hold them together, proving that they are exactly the same size!

14

Falling coin

THE TRICK

Make a coin resting over a bottle neck on a toothpick fall into the bottle without touching coin, toothpick or bottle.

Preparation

You will need:
- a toothpick
- a small coin
- a bottle with a neck wide enough to take the coin
- water

! **Make sure the coin does not hold the toothpick in place. The lighter the coin, the easier it is for the toothpick to move. Instead of a toothpick you can also use a wooden coffee stirrer.**

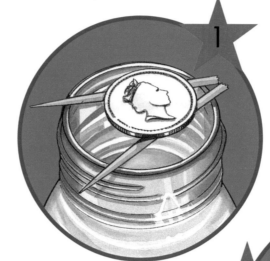

Bend the toothpick in two but do not break it completely. Put it on the top of the bottle and put the coin on the toothpick. Challenge anyone to get the coin into the bottle without touching coin, toothpick or bottle.

When everyone else gives up, all you have to do is allow a few drops of water to fall onto the broken part of the toothpick.

Much to everyone's surprise, the toothpick will begin to straighten up, and soon it will allow the coin to fall into the bottle.

SCIENCE

The wood from which the toothpick is made consists of very fine, straw-like fibres. The water is absorbed by these fibres causing them to swell, and the swelling causes the two halves of the toothpick to move. Plants get water from their roots to their leaves through very fine tubes in the roots, stems and branches in the same way. This absorption of water is known as capillary action. On pages 10-11 you can find another trick that is based on capillary action.

Roll up

THE TRICK

A round box defies gravity by rolling up a slope instead of rolling down...

(!) Make sure you test how heavy the weight in the box should be for it to work properly. Another thing to test is the steepness of the card slope.

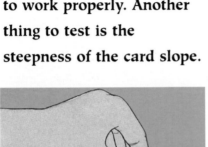

Preparation

You will need:
- a round box (a cheese box is ideal)
- a heavy weight or stone
- some modelling clay
- stiff card and a small box to make a slope

1 Use the modelling clay to fix the stone inside the box and then put the lid on.
2 Paint the box.
3 Put a small pencil dot on the outside of the box to show you where the weight is.

Put the sheet of card against the small box to create a slope.

Show the round box and place it on the sloping surface. Make sure that the pencil dot is at the top and slightly forwards. Tell your audience you can defy gravity and make the box roll uphill.

Top Tip

The moment the box falls off the slope, it will rock a bit. This can be a giveaway that there is a weight inside the box. To avoid your audience finding out what made your trick work, it is important to catch the box the moment it falls off the slope, so it won't rock. Find the longest distance your box can roll by practising. The further your box rolls, the more impressive the trick will be!

When you let go, the box will, to everyone's surprise, roll uphill instead of down!

3

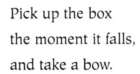

4 Pick up the box the moment it falls, and take a bow.

SCIENCE

Everything is attracted to Earth by a force called gravity.

Normally this force would pull an empty box downhill. In the trick, you put a weight at the top of the box, slightly forwards. The force of gravity working on the weight is bigger than the force of gravity pulling the box downhill. This causes the box to roll uphill. For the box to roll downhill, the weight would have to be slightly backwards at the top of the box.

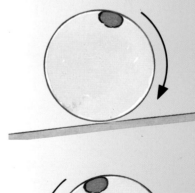

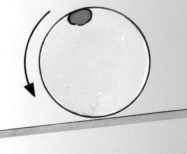

Egg suspension

THE TRICK

An ordinary egg in a bowl of water will sink to the bottom. Use some of your special magic powder to make it float!

2 You can write 'Magic Powder' on the box if you like.

3 Fill the box with salt.

Preparation

You will need:
- a small box
- lots of salt
- a fresh egg
- a clear bowl
- a jug of water

1 Decorate a small box to make a magic container for the salt.

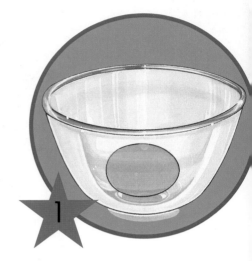

Put the egg in the bowl and ask your audience if they think it will float or sink when you fill the bowl with water. Some people will say, "Float", and some will say, "Sink".

Take the jug and pour water into the bowl. The egg will stay at the bottom. Say that those who thought the egg would sink were right, but then you can use your magic powder to make the egg float, and prove the others right too!

DID YOU KNOW...

... that some dinosaurs laid eggs? *Maiasaura* mums dug out nests as big as paddling pools, then laid about twenty eggs! She stayed around until they hatched and fed the babies shoots and tender leaves until they were big enough to venture out alone.

3 Take the box of salt and while you say some magic words, pour the salt into the bowl.

4 The egg will start to float, and you have now proved everyone right!

SCIENCE

Whether an object sinks or floats depends on its density. One cupful of water, for example, is lighter than one cupful of egg, so the density of the egg is greater than the density of the water. This means the egg will sink in water. When you add salt, the water becomes more dense than normal water, and more dense than the egg. This means the egg will not sink in salt water, but will rise to the surface.

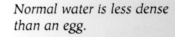
Normal water is less dense than an egg.

Salty water is denser than an egg.

Out from under

THE TRICK

A coin is trapped under a glass tumbler. You get it out from under the tumbler without even touching it.

Preparation

> **You will need:**
> • a tablecloth or a tea towel
> • one thin coin
> • two thick coins
> • a tumbler
> • a handkerchief

Put the tablecloth or tea towel on the table where you will perform.

Put the three coins in a row on the table, with the thin one between the other two. Place the tumbler over the centre coin with the rim of the tumbler resting on the two thicker coins.

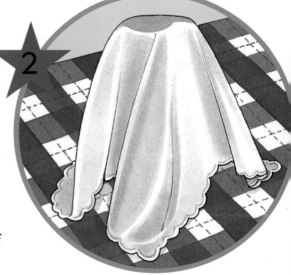

Cover the tumbler with the handkerchief. Say that you are going to get the coin out from beneath the tumbler without touching the tumbler, the handkerchief or the coins.

SCIENCE

If you looked at the coin and the material under under a microscope, you would see their surfaces are made up of lots of 'hills and valleys'. These lock when one object is dragged over the other. This is called friction. It makes the coin 'stick' to the material and move towards you when you scratch. When the material springs back, however, the material moves much faster than when you scratch. This means the material and the coin lose their grip on each other and the material 'slips' underneath the coin. If you scratch enough times, the coin will creep out from beneath the tumbler.

3

While you are saying this, secretly scratch your fingernail against the tablecloth. Do this with your finger behind the tumbler so the audience cannot see what you are up to. The coin will slowly creep out from the tumbler.

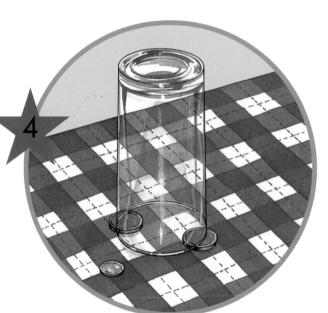

4

When you see the coin, stop scratching and move away from the table. Get someone from your audience to lift the handkerchief so everyone can see that the coin really is away from the tumbler.

Top Tip

• When you do this trick, you have to make sure the audience cannot hear you scratching. Test the trick on the table you will actually perform it on, because the scratching sounds louder on some tables than on others. You can also disguise the noise by having music on while you perform, or prepare some patter for while you scratch.

• Instead of a handkerchief, you can use a silk if you have one to create a more magical effect.

Abnormal arrow

THE TRICK

Draw an arrow on a piece of paper and make it change direction using just a glass of water.

Preparation

You will need:
- a piece of paper
- a marker pen
- a straight-sided glass tumbler
- a jug of water

There is no special preparation for this trick, but keep in mind that it is only really suitable for showing to one person at a time.

Hand the piece of paper and marker pen to the spectator and ask him to draw a horizontal arrow.

Now it is time to let your magic powers work. Pour some water into the tumbler. Make sure it will be as high as the arrow on the piece of paper.

DID YOU KNOW...
... that of all the water in the world only about 3 per cent is fresh water? Of that 3 per cent, about three-quarters is frozen in glaciers and in icecaps. Glaciers and icecaps contain as much water as flows in all the rivers on Earth in 1,000 years!

SCIENCE

When light passes from one medium to another, it bends. This is called refraction. In the trick, light passes from air through glass, through water, again through glass and again through air before it reaches your eye. This means the water and the glass bend the light before it reaches your eye. It gets bent so much that the point of the arrow seems to be at the opposite side of where it really is.

Put the piece of paper behind the tumbler and ask the spectator to look through the tumbler and tell you which way the arrow points.

Say you can make the arrow point the other way without turning the piece of paper. Say some magic words and slowly move the piece of paper backwards while the spectator keeps looking through the tumbler. Right before his eyes the arrow will soon point the other way!

The Möbius strip

THE TRICK

Cut 3 rings of paper down the centre, and produce 3 different end results...

Preparation

You will need:
- 3 long strips of paper, each about 50 cm long and 5 cm wide
- glue
- scissors

1 Take one strip and glue the ends together to form a loop.

2 Take the second strip and give half a turn to the end of the paper before gluing the ends together.

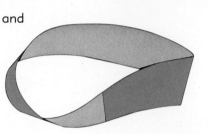

3 Before gluing the ends of the third strip together, twist the paper for one complete turn.

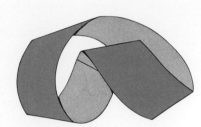

Tell the audience how you can make some paper rings do very strange things. Take the first ring and cut it all the way down the centre.

You will have two paper loops – just as one would expect. Say that this was a warm-up and that you will now use your magic powers to make the next ring do something unexpected. Take the second loop and cut it down through the centre.

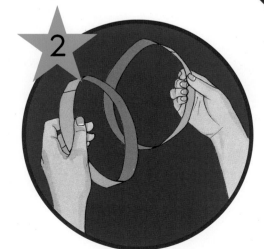

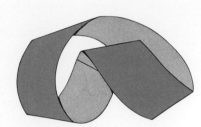

This time you will have one large loop!

4 When you cut the third ring through the centre, to everyone's amazement, you end up with two loops linked together!

IT'S mAGic

Maths magic
Magicians call this trick 'The Afghan Bands', but it is actually a Möbius strip, which was discovered by the German mathematician Augustus Ferdinand Möbius (1790-1868). The great American magician Harry Blackstone Sr (1885-1965) was the first to feature this trick in his act and got a great deal of audience appreciation from it.

SCIENCE

This is a trick of mathematics. This is how it works.
If you tape the two ends of a strip of paper together without twisting, you will get two separate paper rings when you cut down the middle and halve. If you give the strip half a twist, you are connecting part of red, and part of blue together. When you cut it through the middle you make what is, in fact, an 8-shape, which is a big loop.

Finally, if you give the strip a whole twist, before taping the ends together, you are connecting colour to colour. But when you cut down the middle you have two circles, one red and one blue that are linked together because of the whole twist.

Strong

THE TRICK

In this impressive trick, you prove that you are stronger than four other people together!

Preparation

You will need:
• two brooms (or broom handles)
• about 10 metres of rope

Get two people to hold each end of a broomstick horizontally at arm's length. Opposite them have two other people hold the other broomstick the same way. The two couples should face each other about a metre apart.

Top Tip

• Because you need a lot of room for this trick, it is probably best to perform it outside.
• You can ask for volunteers who think they are stronger than you are. Have them hold the broomsticks. Or you may ask spectators to feel your arm muscles and ask them if they think you are stronger than four people. Unless you are very muscular, they will be very impressed when you pull the two brooms together.

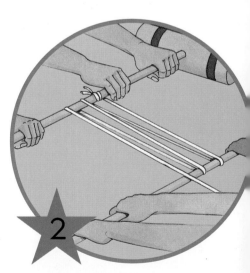

Explain that you will prove you a stronger than the four of them together. Now tie one end of the rope to one of the broomsticks ar wind it five or six times round bo brooms. Make sure the rope doe: not cross itself.

DID YOU KNOW...

... that ropes are made up of lots of small strands? They are twisted together to make the rope stronger. If one of the strands snaps, many others still work together to keep the rope from breaking.

Ask the four people to try and keep the broomsticks apart, while you will try and pull them together. Stand behind one of the pairs and start pulling steadily.

Despite the fact that you are pitting your strength against four people, you will be able to pull the two broomsticks – and the people holding them – together!

By winding the rope around the two broomsticks, you have created a pulley system. This reduces the amount of effort you need to lift an object. In the trick, this means you need less effort to pull the broomsticks together. By winding the rope around the brooms several times, you will need to pull more rope, but you will need less effort to pull the broomsticks together.

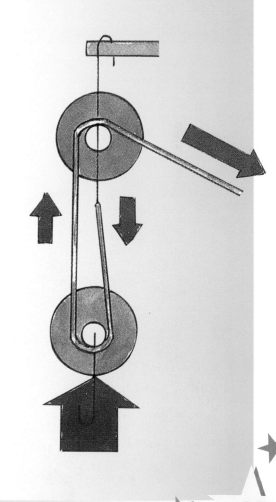

Spin and spin again

THE TRICK

When a spectator stops a spinning egg, it remains – as everyone would expect – stationary. When you do this, the egg stops, then magically continues to spin by itself!

Preparation

> **You will need:**
> • two eggs

1 Ask an adult to boil one of the eggs. Let it cool down.
2 Mark it with a small pencil dot so you know which egg is raw and which is boiled.

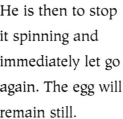

Hand the boiled egg to a spectator and ask him to spin it on its side.

He is then to stop it spinning and immediately let go again. The egg will remain still.

Ancient magic

Magic based on science has been around for a very long time. One of the earliest examples of magic we know about was at the Temple of Hercules at Tyre almost 2,000 years ago, when mirrors were used to produce images of the gods. Some ancient temples had doors that opened magically when a fire was lit on an altar. What the awe-struck worshippers did not know was that the heat from the fire caused air inside the altar to expand. This forced water from a container beneath the altar into a bucket. As the bucket got heavier, it pulled a series of pulleys that operated the temple doors.

IT'S MAGIC

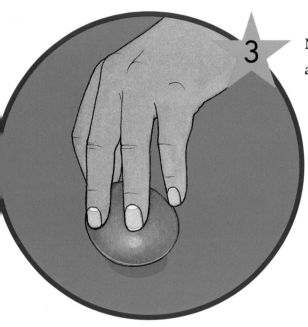

3 Now say you have total control over an egg and can keep it spinning for a while even after you stop it. Take the raw egg and spin it.

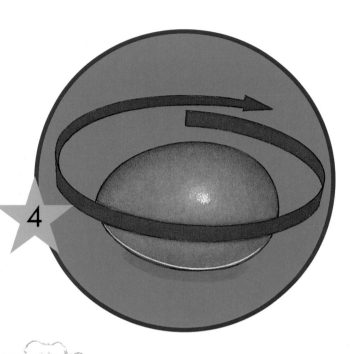

4

Stop the egg just like the spectator did. Let go immediately and, to everyone's amazement, the egg will continue to spin.

SCIENCE

Whether an egg keeps spinning or not after you stop it depends on what is inside it. The raw egg is liquid inside and the boiled one is solid. That's where the secret to this trick lies. When you stop the raw egg from spinning, the liquid inside will continue to spin for a little while longer, so when you let go, the egg appears to spin of its own accord. The boiled egg has a solid inside, which stops spinning as soon as you stop the egg.

29

Underwater escape

THE TRICK

A paper clip is dropped into a full bottle of water. You hold the bottle behind your back and take out the paper clip without spilling any of the water.

Preparation

You will need:
- a strong magnet
- a bottle full of water
- a paper clip

Before you start, put the magnet in your back pocket where you can get hold of it without anyone knowing.

SCIENCE

Most magnets are made of steel and attract metal. Objects that are attracted to magnets are called magnetic. A magnet has a 'field' around it (see below) where the magnetic force works. This field goes through glass and water, so the paper clip is still attracted to the magnet.

magnetic field

1 Show the bottle of water and the paper clip. Drop the paper clip into the bottle. Announce that you will use your magic powers to get the clip out of the bottle without tipping out any water.

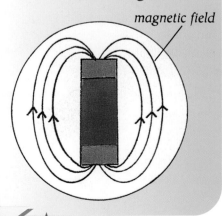

2 Hold the bottle behind your back and 'steal' – secretly get hold of – the magnet. Place the magnet against the side of the bottle at the bottom and draw it up the bottle. Do this very slowly.

3 The clip will be attracted to the magnet and can be drawn up the bottle. Eventually the clip will be out of the bottle and sticking to the magnet.

Remove the paper clip, hide the magnet, and then show the audience both the clip and the bottle.

4

Quelling a revolution

In 1856, the French magician Robert-Houdin (below) was called from retirement by the French government to help quell an uprising in North Africa. They thought using magic would impress the local people. For this, Robert-Houdin used his 'light and heavy chest'. This was a small chest that could not be lifted by even the strongest man unless the magician willed it. The chest was actually controlled by a large electro-magnet hidden beneath the stage.

Index

Glossary of magic words

Patter
The talk with which a magician or other entertainer accompanies a routine.
Props
Any apparatus used by the performer. The word is short for properties.

Silk
A handkerchief or square made of coloured silk.
Steal
To secretly obtain an object from a hiding place.

Websites and clubs

Have you caught the magic bug and want to know more? Here are some magic websites and addresses of clubs you could join:

•www.repromagic.co.uk
A list of clubs across the British Isles.

Magic tricks can be bought from:
•www.merlinswakefield.co.uk
•www.internationalmagic.com
•www.magictricks.com

• www.themagiccircle.co.uk
Site of the famous Magic Circle. Includes a virtual tour of some the club headquarters. The Magic Circle has a club:
Young Magicians' Club
Centre for the Magic Arts
12, Stephenson Way
London NW1 2HD
www.youngmagiciansclub.co.uk

•www.pauldaniels.co.uk – Biography and pictures of Britain's most famous magician.